CONTENTS

Foreword .... *v*

The Promised Messiah^{as}—The Champion of Islam 3
Nanak – A Saint 15
The Revealed Sermon 21
The Great Religious Conference 25
Jesus^{as} in Kashmir 31
In Honour of a Guest 39
The Blessed Rice 43
Healing by Prayer 47
A Debate with Christians 51
Hazrat Ahmad^{as} in Court 57
The Dagger of Muhammad^{saw} 65
The Fate of Sa'dullah 73
The Truth Prevails 77
A Hindu Tries to Hypnotise
Hazrat Ahmad^{as} 83
And God Signed in Red Ink 87
Two Great Martyrs 91
The Girl with Swollen Eyes 99

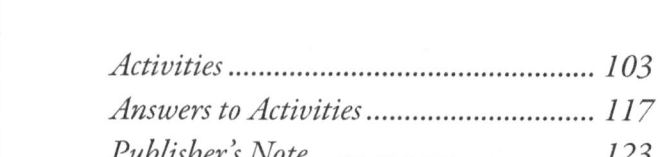

Activities *103*
Answers to Activities *117*
Publisher's Note *123*

FOREWORD

Storytelling remains one of history's most relished pastimes. It inspires its audience to imagine, aspire and dream. Over time, however, elements of exaggeration and fabrication creep in to create a more exhilarating episode, resulting in greater myth than matter of fact.

Stories of early Ahmadiyyat share unique aspects of both. They are strictly based on facts, but their fascinating outcomes, against all odds, dazzle the mind. The reality is that they prove the existence of the Unseen Lord and the support He provides to those who strive in His cause, irrespective of the opposition they face.

Stories from Early Ahmadiyyat is a children's book to remind our youth of the humble origins of the Ahmadiyya Muslim Jama'at at a time when they have grown accustomed to seeing its tremendous international progress and advancement. This success did not come without the sacrifices of humble men and women who trusted in their Lord and the Promised Messiah[as] whom He sent.

Essentially, this book seeks to inspire our youth to adopt the path of righteousness regardless of the obstacles and temptations that lie in their way, in the hopes

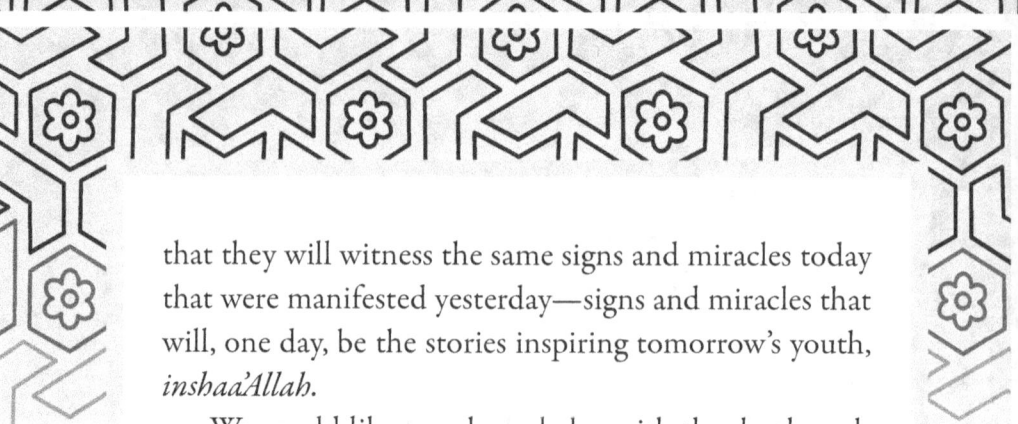

that they will witness the same signs and miracles today that were manifested yesterday—signs and miracles that will, one day, be the stories inspiring tomorrow's youth, *inshaa'Allah*.

We would like to acknowledge with thanks the valuable help of Munawar Ahmed Saeed, Waseem Ahmad Sayed, Myra Ahtesham, Syed Faraz Hussain, Naser-ud-Din Shams, Ayesha Noor, Zulfiqar Ahmad Abbasi, Ahmad Nooruddeen Jahangeerkhan, and Sehrish Ahmed. May Allah the Almighty reward them for their hard work and bless them in this world and in the Hereafter. *Aameen.*

Munir-ud-Din Shams
Additional Wakeelut-Tasneef, London
July 2017

STORIES FROM EARLY AHMADIYYAT

THE PROMISED MESSIAH [as] — THE CHAMPION OF ISLAM

The year 1835 occupies a unique place in the present era of human history; for in that year, a child was born in a small village in the north of India, who was to be appointed by God to be the Messiah and Mahdi. The name of that child was Mirza Ghulam Ahmad. He was Persian by descent and belonged to a noble Mughal family of the Punjab. The family had emigrated from Samarkand in Central Asia to India during the reign of Babar, the founder of the Mughal Empire in India. The family settled in a place called Islampur which later came to be known as Islampur Qaazi; it was so called because it was the resident town of the first ancestor of Mirza Ghulam Ahmad who came to India and was appointed as *Qaazi* (magistrate) over 70 villages around Islampur. Later, it came to be known as Qadian.

Ignorance prevailed all aorund. Not many people in that part of India were fond of learning. Only a few could read and write. There was no post office in Qadian, no link with other parts of the country by rail or road. The nearest town was Batala, which was about 12 miles away. For several generations the family held offices of respectability and honour under the government, but when the Sikhs came into power, the family estate was reduced to a few villages. A noble Sikh leader, Maharaja Ranjit Singh, restored some of it back to the family; but during the British rule, the land was again confiscated and all its privileges forfeited, except for proprietary rights over Qadian and a few surrounding villages. It was in this remote village that Mirza Ghulam Ahmad grew up as a young boy.

As he belonged to a well-to-do family, tutors were engaged for his education. They taught him to read the Holy Quran and gave him elementary instruction in Arabic and Persian, Logic, Philosophy, and Grammar. His father, Hazrat Mirza Ghulam Murtaza, was a renowned physician, and had his own library. Young Mirza Ghulam Ahmad would often go into the library and spend most of his time reading books. He loved reading books in seclusion. He loved the Holy Quran and the mosque. He would remain absorbed for hours in the Holy Book and passed most of his time in the mosque, engaged in deep thought and contemplation, offering prayers to Allah for the grant of a true understanding of the Holy Quran.

He had learned to swim and ride at an early age, but

his principal form of exercise was brisk walking; he kept to it throughout his life. Observing his seclusion, his father grew very apprehensive about him. He thought that if his son did not take interest in the management of the family estate or secure a good government job, he would be unable to provide for himself in the future. With these considerations in mind, he would often urge his son to take up either of these occupations, but the young Mirza Ghulam Ahmad did not like these jobs. However, out of regard for his father's wishes, he occupied himself with the management of the family estate and often visited Batala for litigation. Later, he also obtained a government job in the city of Sialkot. Whilst in Sialkot, he came into contact with Christian missionaries and often engaged himself in religious discussions with them. Those who came in contact with him admired him very much for his sincerity, scholarship, and moral excellence.

In 1868, Mirza Ghulam Ahmad's mother passed away; his father sent a messenger to him with the sad news and a request that he resign his position and return to Qadian. Thus, after four years stay in Sialkot, he gave up his job and came back to Qadian. Here, once again, he occupied himself with the management of the family estate, but his heart was not in worldly affairs. Most of his time was spent in reading the Holy Book, Traditions of the Holy Prophet^{saw}, and books on mysticism. This period in his life was marked by his devotion to prayers and fasting. Under a Divine inspiration, he observed fasts continually for eight or nine months, which largely added to his spiritual experience.

He frequently experienced true dreams which he recounted to the residents of Qadian who knew him and kept his company; Hindus and Muslims alike. These dreams always came true and those people to whom he related them became witnesses of their truth. Then, one day in 1876, God revealed to him that his father would pass away in the evening. His father was on his sick bed and the thought of being without his father shook young Mirza Ghulam Ahmad. He told others about what had been revealed to him, and all of them were witness to the fact that the prophecy was fulfilled shortly afterwards. Up until then, Mirza Ghulam Ahmad was fully dependent upon his father, but after his father's death, he would no longer have his support. Suddenly, another revelation came to him:

اَلَيْسَ اللّٰهُ بِكَافٍ عَبْدَهٗ

Is not God sufficient for His servant?

Thus God consoled him and assured him of His continued help.

Mirza Ghulam Ahmad[as] married twice. He had two sons from his first marriage—Mirza Sultan Ahmad and Mirza Fazal Ahmad. Later, he married Nusrat Jahaan Begum[ra], a respectable lady from the family of Khawaja Mir Dard. Other than those who died in infancy, Mirza Ghulam Ahmad[as] had five children—three sons and two daughters—from this marriage.

When Mirza Ghulam Ahmad[as] saw that Islam was being attacked from all sides, he was much perturbed. In those days, the Christian missionaries, financed by the great Western Powers, were trying their utmost to destroy Islam. Hindu sects, especially the Aryah Samaj and the Brahmu Samaj also stood up against Islam. The Aryah Samaj was the most aggressive; it produced abusive literature against Islam in which attacks were made on the character of the Holy Prophet, Hazrat Muhammad[saw]. Mirza Ghulam Ahmad[as] took his pen and started writing in defence of Islam. The very first book he wrote was *Baraaheen-e-Ahmadiyya*, in which he upheld the truth of Islam and replied to all the objections raised by the opponents of Islam. The book was regarded as a masterpiece, an example of which could not be found in the entire history of Islam. Hazrat Ahmad[as] wrote more than ninety books on various religious topics.

In the year 1882, while he was busy writing, Hazrat Ahmad[as] saw in a vision that the Holy Prophet Muhammad[saw] embraced him. He felt as if bright rays were emanating from the face of the Holy Prophet[saw] and entering into his own body. This vision was followed by a revelation:

يَا أَحْمَدُ بَارَكَ اللّٰهُ فِيكَ، مَا رَمَيْتَ إِذْ رَمَيْتَ وَلٰكِنَّ اللّٰهَ رَمٰى، الرَّحْمٰنُ عَلَّمَ الْقُرْآنَ، لِتُنْذِرَ قَوْمًا مَّا أُنْذِرَ آبَاؤُهُمْ، وَلِتَسْتَبِيْنَ سَبِيْلُ الْمُجْرِمِيْنَ. قُلْ إِنِّىْ أُمِرْتُ وَأَنَا أَوَّلُ الْمُؤْمِنِيْنَ.

Allah has placed blessing in you, O Ahmad. Whatever you did let loose, it was not you but it was Allah who let it loose. Allah has taught you the Quran so that you should warn the people whose ancestors have not been warned, and that the way of the guilty ones might become manifest. Say: 'I have been commissioned and I am the first of the believers.'

It was with this revelation that he was commissioned by God to reform the world and was told that he was indeed the Messiah that had been promised to the world.

On the 12th of January 1889, he established the Ahmadiyya Muslim Jama'at. Incidentally, this was the date of birth of the Promised Son, Mirza Bashir-ud-Din

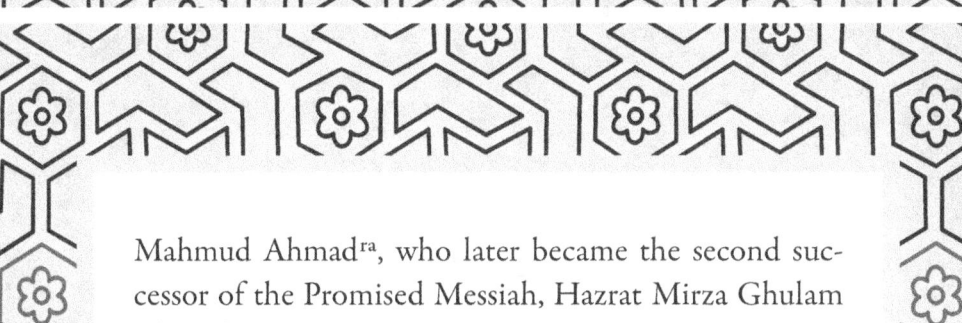

Mahmud Ahmad[ra], who later became the second successor of the Promised Messiah, Hazrat Mirza Ghulam Ahmad[as].

There was a popular belief among the Muslims in those days that Jesus[as] Christ was alive in the heavens and that he would descend in the latter days. God revealed to Hazrat Ahmad[as] that Jesus[as] had died a natural death and that the prophecy about his second advent did not mean that Jesus[as] himself would come back to this world. He told the world that Jesus[as] was buried in Kashmir in India. He collected evidence to show that the people of Kashmir were the descendants of Jews who had migrated there in the days of Nebuchadnezzar, and that Jesus[as] travelled from Palestine to India. He sent a delegation to Kashmir to make a thorough investigation of this matter, on the basis of which Hazrat Ahmad[as] wrote a book *Masih Hindustaan Mein, [Jesus in India]*. Quite a number of European writers and other researchers have also concluded that the people of Kashmir are the descendants of Jews and that Jesus[as] did travel to that part of the world in search of the lost tribes of Israel. Proofs have also become available that Jesus[as] did not die on the cross. After his wounds healed, he left Palestine and went to other lands.

Hazrat Ahmad[as] also claimed that God had revealed

to him that he was the Messiah who had been promised to the world. He supported his claim by various verses of the Holy Quran, Traditions of the Holy Prophet[saw] of Islam, visions and revelations of many great Muslim saints, as well as religious and historical records of the past.

God also revealed to him that he had been raised in the spirit of all the bygone Prophets and made him announce that he was the Messiah for Christians, Mahdi for Muslims, Krishna for Hindus, Buddha for Buddhists and a counter-part of all the previous prophets; a Redeemer for the whole of humanity.

His claim to be the Messiah and Mahdi created a huge storm of opposition from Muslims, Christians, and others. The so-called learned among the Muslims issued decrees (fatwas), declaring him to be an infidel (kafir). In fact all the opponents joined hands to oppose the Promised Messiah[as] and to destroy his cause. They tried their utmost to stop the growth of the Ahmadiyya Muslim Jama'at. They tried all those tactics used by the opponents of the holy Prophets of God. The followers of Hazrat Ahmad[as] were intimidated or ex-communicated. Life was made hard for them. Wives were forcibly separated from their husbands. Many Ahmadis were even murdered and some stoned to death. The Promised

Messiah[as] himself was drawn into litigation and falsely charged with heinous crimes. But the Promised Messiah[as] was declared innocent in the cases filed against him, and all such efforts failed to stop the progress of the Movement.

He, on the other hand, intensified his efforts in proclaiming the truth of Islam; removing the doubts and clarifying the accusations made against him and Islam. His writings gained momentum and he entered into many debates with his opponents in defence of Islam. God Almighty had assured him of his final victory and gave him the glad tidings that people in all corners of the world would enter the fold of Islam through the Ahmadiyya Muslim Jama'at. Thus, in spite of all the opposition, the hearts of men and women began to be drawn towards the Holy Founder of the Ahmadiyya Muslim Jama'at. Whoever came in contact with him or read his books was deeply impressed by the truth of his claim. Thus his followers grew to hundreds of thousands in number. After the death of the Promised Messiah[as], the work of the propagation of Islam was carried on by his successors. Everyday missions throughout the globe are spreading the message of Ahmadiyyat, the true Islam and the Community is growing day by day.

Towards the end of the year 1905, the Promised Messiah[as] received a number of revelations which foretold that his end was fast approaching. On October 18, 1905, he saw a new earthen vessel containing a small quantity of clear water at the bottom of it, not more than two or three draughts. The revelation of God said:

آبِ زندگی
Water of life

Meaning thereby that only two or three years of his life were left.

In view of these revelations, the Promised Messiah[as] thought it advisable to write a few lines by way of advice and guidance to his followers; the pamphlet is known as *al-Wasiyyat* [*The Will*]. In it he asserted that the Ahmadiyya Muslim Jama'at would continue to flourish and that a second manifestation of God's power would commence after his death. He specifically mentioned the name of Hazrat Abu Bakr[ra] to indicate that the second manifestation would take the form of *Khilaafat* (Succession). We are blessed that the Jama'at is now continuing to make progress under the fifth Khalifa of the Promised Messiah[as].

In April 1908, he went to Lahore, the capital of Punjab. He was busy writing a book, *Paighaam-e-Sulh* [*The Message of Peace*], when he suddenly fell ill. It was on 26 May 1908, with the words 'Allah, my Ever Dear and Loving Allah' on his lips, that he breathed his last at the age of 73.

$$\text{إِنَّا لِلَّهِ وَإِنَّا إِلَيْهِ رَاجِعُونَ}$$

Surely, to Allah we belong and to Him shall we return.[1]

His body was carried to Qadian the next day, where he was laid to rest. Hazrat Ahmad[as] had spent his life in the service of Islam. He upheld its doctrines and established its superiority over other religions. He gave the true interpretation of the Holy Quran, removed all the misunderstandings and false beliefs which had crept into the Islamic faith with the passage of time, re-established faith in the Living God, and laid bare the unacceptable doctrines of other religions. He was indeed the Champion of Islam. May God shower His blessings upon him.

Questions

QUESTION 1: When was Hazrat Ahmad[as] born?

---

1. A phrase from the Holy Quran which is recited by Muslims to express their deepest sorrow.

YOUR RESPONSE: _____

QUESTION 2: What was Hazrat Ahmad's[as] principal form of exercise?

YOUR RESPONSE: _____

_____

QUESTION 3: What was the name of the first book written by Hazrat Ahmad[as]?

YOUR RESPONSE: _____

_____

QUESTION 4: When did Hazrat Ahmad[as] establish the Ahmadiyya Muslim Jama'at?

YOUR RESPONSE: _____

_____

QUESTION 5: When did Hazrat Ahmad[as] pass away?

YOUR RESPONSE: _____

NANAK – A SAINT

In the year 1895, Hazrat Ahmad^{as} announced that Hazrat Guru Nanak, commonly known as the founder of the Sikh religion, was in fact a great Muslim Saint. He produced evidence from the Sikh scriptures of the fact that Nanak converted to Islam in the latter part of his life.

Nanak was born into a Hindu family of Talwandi in the Sheikhupura district of the Punjab. The village is now known as Nankana Sahib i.e. the birth place of Nanak. His father, Kaloo Ram, provided for him the means of education that was in vogue at that time. He studied Persian from some Muslim teachers and also learnt some Islamic principles from them. He soon found that the teachings of the Vedas did not satisfy him, so he searched for a path which could lead him directly to God. He looked for a guide who could show him such a path. He found one such guide in the person of a Muslim saint of the Chishti Order of Sufis, and he gladly became a Muslim, pledging himself at the saint's hands. Nanak concealed the fact of his conversion for some time, and practiced his faith in privacy. But he could not remain quiet for long. Eventually, he declared that he was a Muslim and preferred the society of Muslim scholars.

Nanak was now a changed man. He travelled far and wide and visited Muslim Shrines. It is said that he also undertook the long journey to Mecca and Medina and performed the Hajj. He also visited some other places that are sacred to Muslims. He composed verses in praise of Allah and the Holy Prophet Muhammad[saw]. As a visible sign of his belief, he used to wear a cloak on which some verses of the Holy Quran were written. Another proof of his conversion to Islam is the fact that he married a Muslim girl.

The Sikhs regard Nanak as the founder of Sikhism, and love him dearly. They collected his sayings and verses in the form of a book, called the Granth Sahib, and hold it in high esteem; but they do not consider him a Muslim, in spite of all his verses in praise of the Holy Prophet[saw] of Islam. The *cholah* (the cloak which Nanak wore) is reverently preserved at Dera Baba Nanak, in the Gurdaspur District. The cloak was made of cotton and had a certain number of writings worked into its fabric. The Sikh belief was that this cloak had been sent down from heaven by God Almighty as a mark of honour for Nanak, and as a means of providing security for him against all danger.

When Hazrat Ahmad[as] learned of the cloak at Dera Baba Nanak and heard rumours about its divine origin,

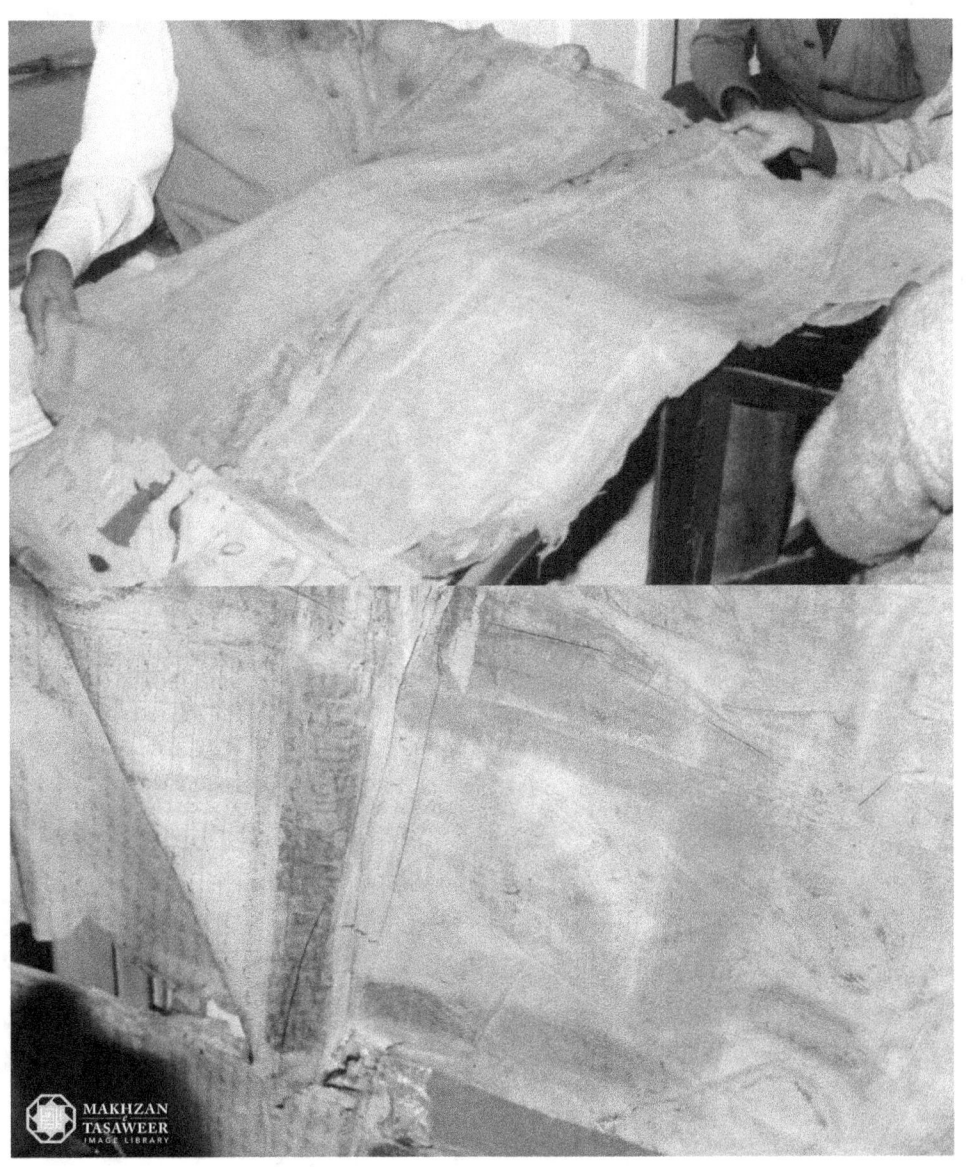

Cholah (the cloak which Guru Nanak wore)

he became anxious to discover the significance of this relic. Hazrat Ahmad[as] therefore sent a delegation of four of his followers to see the cloak. They reported that the writings on the cloak were the verses of the Holy Quran, written in Arabic. The writings also contained the Kalimah: لَا إِلٰهَ إِلَّا اللهُ مُحَمَّدٌ رَسُوْلُ اللهِ ['There is no one worthy of worship except Allah, Muhammad is the Messenger of Allah'].

Hazrat Ahmad[as] was greatly pleased to hear this report, as it was a grand proof that Nanak was a Muslim saint. He decided to pay a visit to Dera Baba Nanak himself. On 30th September 1895, he visited the temple accompanied by ten of his followers, and made a request to the keeper of the relic to let them view the sacred cloak. It was discovered that the cloak was wrapped in about 300 coverings of silk, cotton, and the finest wool. Some of them bore the name and description of the donor. These covers were removed one by one. The process took more than an hour and, in the end, the cloak was finally exposed in its full glory. It was revealed to be a blessed fabric that was inscribed with the Islamic *Kalimah* and several verses of the Holy Quran, including the opening chapter (*Surah al-Faatihah*). No un-Islamic writing was present on the cloak.

The cloak was spread out before the eyes of the visitors and, under the direction of Hazrat Ahmad, the

Promised Messiah[as], a sketch was made of the cloak and of the writings that appeared on it. Hazrat Ahmad[as] related the whole story about the cloak in his book *Satt Bachan* [*True Word*]. The publication generated great interest in the Sikh community and several members joined the Ahmadiyya Muslim Jama'at.

Some time later, Hazrat Ahmad[as] learnt that a book which was very dear to Nanak was also preserved in a *gurdawaarah* at Guru Har Sahai in the Ferozepur District. It was known as the *Pothi* (Prayer Book) of Baba Nanak. Hazrat Ahmad[as] sent three of his followers to investigate. It turned out to be a copy of the Holy Quran.

In fact, Nanak lived and died a Muslim, as declared by Hazrat Ahmad[as]. His funeral prayers were offered by a large number of Muslims.

Questions

QUESTION 1: Who was Baba Nanak?

YOUR RESPONSE: _____

_____

QUESTION 2: What was the name of his father?

YOUR RESPONSE: _____

QUESTION 3: Where was he born?

YOUR RESPONSE: _____

QUESTION 4: How did he convert to Islam?

YOUR RESPONSE: _____

_____

QUESTION 5: What do these terms mean? (a) Granth Sahib; (b) Cholah.

YOUR RESPONSE: _____

_____

QUESTION 6: Why do you think Baba Nanak was a Muslim saint?

YOUR RESPONSE: _____

THE REVEALED SERMON

It was the year 1900 when the Promised Messiah[as] delivered a sermon in Arabic, known and published as *Khutbah Ilhaamiyyah* [*The Revealed Sermon*]. As its name indicates, the sermon was Divinely inspired. It must be mentioned that Arabic was not the mother tongue of Hazrat Ahmad[as], nor had he been to places where Arabic was spoken.

One of the charges made against Hazrat Ahmad[as] by his opponents was that he was not well versed in the Arabic language, therefore he could not claim to understand the Holy Quran fully and be able to put forward arguments in support of his claims. Moreover, they said that he had not attended any famous religious schools where this sort of education was supplied. It was true that he did not have any formal school education in Arabic, but God, by His Divine Grace, bestowed upon him the knowledge of the Arabic language. The Promised Messiah[as] himself has written that God had taught him forty thousand root words of the Arabic language in a single night. Thereafter, he was commanded by God to write in Arabic and promised him special help. Accordingly, he wrote one chapter in Arabic, which is printed in his book *Aa'eenah-e-Kamaalaat-e-Islam* [*The Mirror of the Excellences of Islam*]. This chapter was a challenge to those who put forward those charges.

Then, on the day of Eid-ul-Azhaa in 1900, the Promised Messiah[as] announced that God had commanded him to deliver the sermon in Arabic, and that He had granted him the capacity to do so. The Eid prayer was led by Maulawi Abdul Karim[ra]. After the Prayer, the Promised Messiah[as] delivered a short sermon in Urdu. He then asked Hazrat Maulana Noor-ud-Din[ra] and Hazrat Maulawi Abdul Karim[ra] to sit near him and directed: 'Whatever I am going to say now is Divinely inspired, take note of it carefully so that it may be safeguarded, for later, I myself may not be able to recall what I say now.'

Then, he began his speech in Arabic. His eyes were half-closed as if he was in a trance, and his blessed face appeared to glow with Divine light. His forehead radiated bright rays of light that dazzled the eyes of those who looked at it. The delivery of the sermon occupied more than one hour. When he had finished speaking, the audience requested that it should be translated into Urdu, so the Urdu version of this miraculous sermon was given by Maulawi Abdul Karim[ra]. While this was being done, Hazrat Ahmad[as], overtaken by gratitude towards God for the great bounty He had bestowed on him, went into prostration and the whole congregation followed his example.

The Promised Messiah[as] has stated about this revealed sermon:

> Glory be to Allah! At that time a hidden fountain was gushing out. I do not know whether it was I who was speaking or some angel through my tongue, as I knew that I had no share in that speech. Self-formed sentences were coming out of my mouth, and every sentence was a sign from God for me. It is an intellectual miracle displayed by God, and none can present the like of it.

The main topic of the sermon was the philosophy of sacrifice. It stands as a unique example of the deep insight of spiritual values that were bestowed upon him by God Almighty.

Questions

QUESTION 1: In which year did Hazrat Ahmad[as] deliver the revealed sermon?

YOUR RESPONSE: _____

_____

QUESTION 2: Who did Hazrat Ahmad[as] ask to write the sermon as he spoke?

YOUR RESPONSE: _____

_____

QUESTION 3: Who was asked to translate the sermon from Arabic to Urdu?

YOUR RESPONSE: _____

_____

QUESTION 4: What was the main topic of the sermon?

YOUR RESPONSE: _____

_____

THE GREAT RELIGIOUS CONFERENCE

Towards the close of the nineteenth century, a Hindu leader named Swami Sadhu Shugan Chandar and his associates organised a religious conference wherein the followers of different religions could demonstrate the truths and beauties contained in their respective religions. He invited Hazrat Ahmad[as] to participate in the conference to be held in Lahore. Despite ill health Hazrat Ahmad[as] agreed to participate in the conference.

The organisers of the religious conference set up a working committee consisting of Hindu, Muslim, and Christian members. The committee decided to hold the conference on the 26th, 27th, and 28th of December, 1896, at Lahore. Invitations were sent to scholars of various religions, who were to base their speeches on the following five topics:

1. The physical, moral, and spiritual states of man.
2. Life after death.
3. The object of man's life and the means for its attainment.

4. The effect of human actions on life here and hereafter.
5. The sources of Divine knowledge.

Swami Sadhu Shugan Chandar visited Qadian and personally requested Hazrat Ahmad[as] to write a thesis for the conference. Hazrat Ahmad[as] was not feeling well at that time. He prayed to God to grant him the strength to prepare a thesis on the beauties of Islam. By the grace of God, he finished his thesis well in time. God also informed him that his paper would excel all the papers to be read on the occasion.

This prophecy was given wide circulation before the conference. Posters were displayed on walls. Handbills were distributed throughout the country. Hazrat Ahmad's[as] paper was to be read out on 27th December, in the afternoon. Since Hazrat Ahmad[as] could not attend personally due to illness, he appointed one of his disciples, Maulawi Abdul Karim[ra], to read the paper on his behalf. The hall was full to capacity and hundreds of people were standing outside to listen to the speech. Everyone listened with great interest. The time allotted for this paper was two hours, but during this time only a part of the paper was read. Seeing this, Maulawi

Mubarak Ali, who was the next to speak, announced that the time allotted to him for reading the paper could be used for the further reading of Hazrat Ahmad's[as] paper. This announcement was joyfully acclaimed by the audience. But even then, the reading could not be completed. The director of the conference agreed to the suggestion to prolong the session for one hour, but still a part of the paper had yet to be read out. The audience were so deeply interested that they requested the managing committee to extend the conference for another day so that the whole thesis could be heard. The committee agreed and so Maulawi Abdul Karim[ra] read the rest of the thesis on the 29th of December.

Hazrat Ahmad's[as] paper was unanimously acclaimed as the best one read out at the conference. Newspapers and journals wrote long columns in its praise. Thus, the prophecy of Hazrat Ahmad[as] published before the conference was fulfilled. The paper has been published as *Philosophy of the Teachings of Islam*.

Questions:

QUESTION 1: In which year was the great religious conference held?

YOUR RESPONSE: _____

_____

QUESTION 2: Who was the organiser of this conference?

YOUR RESPONSE: _____

_____

QUESTION 3: What were the topics for discussion in this conference?

YOUR RESPONSE: _____

_____

_____

QUESTION 4: What was the prophecy?

YOUR RESPONSE: _____

_____

_____

QUESTION 5: Who read out the paper prepared by Hazrat Ahmad[as]?

YOUR RESPONSE: _____

_____

The Tomb of Jesus[as]

JESUS[as] IN KASHMIR

Hazrat Ahmad[as] removed a great misconception concerning the crucifixion, death, and ascension of Jesus Christ which had taken root among the Muslims and Christians. He announced that Jesus[as] did not die on the cross; rather he survived from the agony of the cross and migrated to Kashmir, India where he died and lays buried. He identified his tomb and wrote a book detailing all the scriptural references and research findings to support his thesis.[1] Due to this proclamation, he encountered strong opposition from Christians, as well as Muslims, whose beliefs were quite the opposite of what he preached.

Hazrat Ahmad[as] announced that Jesus[as] was undoubtedly put on the cross, but did not die there. On the contrary, he became unconscious because of grievous pain and injuries, and was taken down from the cross through the efforts of some of his supporters and sympathisers among the Government officials. It was a common practice in those days to break the legs of the crucified persons and to cause their bodies to hang upon

---

1. A hadith of the Holy Prophet Muhammad[saw] says that Prophet Jesus[as] died at the age of 120.

the cross for several days, so that there would be no possibility of the person remaining alive. The body of Jesus[as] was taken down without his bones being broken, even though the soldiers broke the bones of the other two criminals that were upon crosses close by. His body was handed over to his followers, who laid him in a cave and applied some ointment and herbs to his injuries. Jesus[as] recovered from his injuries after three days and then set out to deliver his message to the other tribes of Israel.

He lived to the age of 120 and died a natural death in Srinagar, Kashmir in India, after completing his mission. From subsequent research, Hazrat Ahmad[as] also traced his tomb to Khanyar, Srinagar where it can still be visited.

Let us now examine the beliefs held by Christians and Muslims in general. Christians believe that Jesus[as] died on the cross, his death atoning for the sins of all who had faith in him. He was then resurrected from death, after which his body ascended to Heaven. Muslims in general entertained a similar belief. They believed that Jesus[as] was not put on the cross but was instead taken to Heaven alive, a phantom having been put on the cross in his place.

The basic doctrine of the Church has been that Jesus[as], being son of God, appeared in human shape to take upon himself the whole burden of the sins of human beings, and to sacrifice his life on the cross, so that mankind might attain salvation. Being the son of God and through his death upon the cross he became 'accursed' for mankind's sake and remained in that state for three days to atone for the sins of mankind. He then came back to life and ascended bodily to Heaven, where he is sitting on the right hand of God. He will descend to earth in the Latter Days. It is interesting to note that the text of the Revised Standard Version of the New Testament no longer mentions the bodily ascension of Jesus[as] to Heaven, because it was not in the original Bible.

Jesus[as] himself had said that he was raised among the Children of Israel particularly for the guidance of the 'Lost Sheep of the house of Israel'. Were it true that he was God and his sole purpose to sacrifice his life to redeem the sins of mankind, he would not have prayed in agony for the cup of death on the cross to be taken away from him. If the death of Jesus[as] upon the cross was the fulfilment of the very purpose for which he had been sent, why did he cry out, 'My God! My God! Why hast Thou forsaken me?'

Had he died on the cross and come back to life again, he would have gone to the centre of the city of Jerusalem and announced his triumph over death. The Jews would have believed in him as son of God if they had seen him come alive from the dead. He did not do so. Instead, he met his disciples in secrecy and convinced them that he was still alive and did not die on the cross.

In fact, the whole body of the doctrine—that salvation is possible only through atonement—is a later innovation and finds no support whatsoever in anything that Jesus[as] said or did. The term 'son of God', which he used, cannot be taken literally as this expression is used in the sacred scriptures in a metaphorical sense for other people. The Bible describes Israel[as] [Jacob] as God's son, even 'first born'. The peacemakers are described as the 'children of God'. Even in the Lord's Prayer, God is addressed as Father.

Jesus[as] had announced that his people would be given a similar sign as was given to the people of the prophet Jonah[as]; for as Jonah was in the whale's belly for three days and three nights, so would Jesus[as] remain three days and three nights in the heart of the earth. Now, Jonah[as] was devoured by the whale alive, remained inside its belly alive, though unconscious, and came out alive. Had Jesus[as] died on the cross there would have been no resemblance between his case and that of Jonah's.

Now we look at the belief held by Muslims in general. They believe that Jesus[as] rose to heaven, is still alive there, and will come back to this world to guide mankind. They cannot furnish any proof from the Holy Quran or from the Sayings of the Holy Prophet[saw] of Islam. The Holy Quran clearly states that all the Prophets before Hazrat Muhammad[saw] had died (*Surah Aal-e-Imraan*, 3:145). Similarly, the Sayings of the Holy Prophet[saw] of Islam establish this fact that Jesus died at the age of 120.

The Holy Quran tells us that Jesus[as] was a prophet of God, raised by God among the children of Israel. Jesus[as] himself had made it clear to his people that he was the last prophet to be raised among the children of Israel, and that if the Jews rejected him, the kingdom of heaven would pass to another people. Thus it happened that prophethood came to an end among the children of Israel and the 'Spirit of Truth' (Muhammad, peace be upon him) was raised among the descendants of Ishmael, their brethren.

The prayer of Jesus[as] that the cup of death on the cross be turned away from him, the agonised cry from the cross, the precautions taken by him when meeting his disciples after his recovery from his injuries, are all consistent with the truth taught by the Holy Quran. Even when the body of Jesus[as] was about to be taken down from the cross and was to be handed over to Joseph of Arimathea, a Roman soldier wounded Jesus[as] in his side with a spear. Blood and water came out of his wound; a clear testimony that Jesus[as] was still alive.

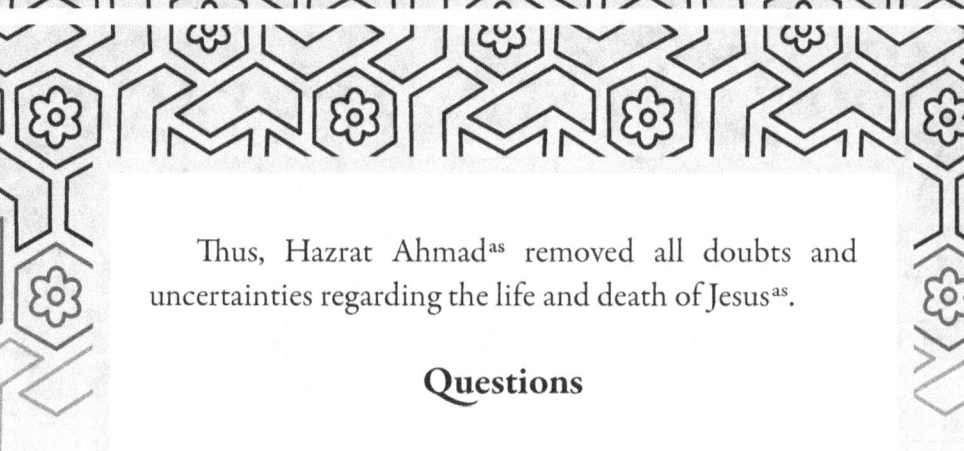

Thus, Hazrat Ahmad[as] removed all doubts and uncertainties regarding the life and death of Jesus[as].

Questions

QUESTION 1: Who announced that Jesus[as] did not die on the cross?

YOUR RESPONSE: _____

_____

QUESTION 2: Where is Jesus[as] buried?

YOUR RESPONSE: _____

_____

QUESTION 3: To what age did Jesus[as] live?

YOUR RESPONSE: _____

_____

QUESTION 4: Give at least one proof from the Holy Quran that Jesus[as] died a natural death

YOUR RESPONSE: _____

IN HONOUR OF A GUEST

Hospitality towards and honouring one's guests are always considered to be the essential trait of a person with high moral characteristics. The Promised Messiah[as] set a splendid example in this respect as well.

Once, one of his companions, Seth Ghulam Nabi[ra], came to Qadian to see him. It was a wet winter's evening, and by the time he arrived, it was quite late. As he had a long tiresome journey, he ate his supper and went to bed immediately. Late at night, someone knocked at the door. He opened the door and was greatly surprised to see the Promised Messiah[as] with a lantern in one hand and a cup of milk in the other. The Promised Messiah[as] apologised for the inconvenience and said affectionately, 'Somebody brought some milk, and it occurred to me that you might be in the habit of drinking hot milk before going to bed; so I have brought a cup for you.' The Companion took the cup from his hand and thanked him. His eyes were full of tears of gratitude.

On another occasion, the Promised Messiah[as] was sitting in his room along with some of his guests when someone knocked on the door. One of the guests moved to open it. The Promised Messiah[as] got up at once and said, 'Wait a bit, I will open the door. You are a guest, and the Holy Prophet[saw] exhorted us to honour our guests.'

What wonderful behaviour! The Messiah of God used to find so much pleasure in entertaining and serving guests.

Questions:

QUESTION 1: Who came to see the Promised Messiah[as] on a wet winter evening?

YOUR RESPONSE: _____

_____

QUESTION 2: To which companion did the Promised Messiah[as] offer milk?

YOUR RESPONSE: _____

_____

QUESTION 3: What did the Promised Messiah[as] offer his companion, Seth Ghulam Nabi?

YOUR RESPONSE: _____

_____

_____

QUESTION 4: Who has exhorted us to honour our guests?

YOUR RESPONSE: _____

_____

_____

_____

THE BLESSED RICE

Once the Promised Messiah[as] invited some of his friends to dinner, but, just when the meal was about to be served, the number of guests increased unexpectedly. So much so that the whole of Mubarak Mosque was full of guests. The Promised Messiah[as] sent word to his wife asking her to send more food. Realising the situation, she became a little worried. She called him in and explained, 'There is only a small quantity of food as it was prepared only for a limited number of guests invited by you. What shall we do now?' The Promised Messiah[as] said very calmly, 'Have no worry, bring the cooking pot to me.' When the cooking pot with rice was brought to him, he covered it with a handkerchief, passed his fingers underneath the cooked rice, and prayed to God. 'Now serve the food to all the guests, God will bless it,' said the Promised Messiah[as], and went out. Accordingly, the food was served. Everyone ate to his fill and there was still some left in the pot.

On another occasion, when Hazrat Ammaa Jaan[ra], the wife of the Promised Messiah[as], prepared some rice specially for him, one of his companions, Nawwab Muhammad Ali Khan[ra], came to see him, along with his family. At dinner time, the Promised Messiah[as] told his wife to serve food for them as well. She said that the quantity of rice was very small; it could not suffice for all. Hearing this, the Promised Messiah[as] approached the cooking pot, said some prayers, blew over it, and said to her, 'Now serve the food in the name of Allah.'

It was reported that the rice was so extra-ordinarily blessed that Nawwab Sahib's family ate to their fill. Some of it was sent to the family of Hazrat Maulana Noor-ud-Din[ra] too. As it soon became known as the 'Blessed Rice', many others came in order to obtain a share of it; and everyone who came was given a portion of it. By the sheer grace of God it proved sufficient for them all.

Questions:

QUESTION 1: Who got worried at the quantity of food for the Promised Messiah's[as] guests?

YOUR RESPONSE: _____

_____

_____

QUESTION 2: What did the Promised Messiah^{as} do to the rice which increased in quantity?

YOUR RESPONSE: _____

_____

_____

QUESTION 3: How much rice did Hazrat Ammaa Jaan make before finding out about the guests at dinner time?

YOUR RESPONSE: _____

_____

_____

QUESTION 4: Who came to visit the Promised Messiah^{as} when the incident of the 'Blessed Rice' occurred?

YOUR RESPONSE: _____

_____

_____

HEALING BY PRAYER

Among the many truths introduced by Hazrat Ahmad[as] is the establishment of the fact that God not only hears the prayers of those who call Him, but also answers them. He said: God has revealed to me more than once that success will be achieved through prayers only. On one occasion, he said: When you stand for prayers, you must believe firmly that your God has power and authority over everything. Then your prayer will be accepted and you will see those miraculous signs of His Power which I have seen. God is a precious treasure; appreciate Him because He can help you at every step.

Following the example set by the Holy Prophet[saw] of Islam, Hazrat Ahmad[as] also used to pray for his people, and there are countless instances of the acceptance of his prayer in a remarkable and extraordinary manner. Here is one example:

There was a student in Ta'lim-ul-Islam High School Qadian, whose name was Abdul Karim. He was the son of a widow who lived in a small village in Hyderabad, South India, nearly sixteen hundred miles from Qadian. While at Qadian, he was bitten by a mad dog. He was immediately taken to Kasauli for treatment in the Pasteur Institute to avert the threat of rabies. Having gone through a full course of treatment there, he returned to Qadian. A few days later, he exhibited signs of hydrophobia. His condition caused great anxiety as he developed the deadly symptoms and began to suffer from the agony of the fatal disease.

Hydrophobia, literally the dread of water, is the main symptom of rabies. The name derives from an aversion to water or other liquids, difficulty in swallowing them and from the violent spasms of the throat which occur when drinking is attempted. Rabies is regarded by the medical profession as a terrible disease in which death is virtually certain.

A telegram was immediately sent to the specialists at Kasauli who had treated him previously, describing his symptoms and asking for directions. A reply was sent back by telegram: 'Sorry, nothing can be done for Abdul Karim.'

Hazrat Ahmad[as] had been advised of the condition of Abdul Karim and was kept informed of the progress of his symptoms. When he was told of the reply received from Kasauli, he was much distressed and was deeply moved out of pity for Abdul Karim and his widowed mother. He prayed to God for his complete recovery. His prayers were accepted and within less than 24 hours Abdul Karim was recovered fully, and he resumed the course of his studies.

Hazrat Ahmad[as] has in fact shown many other similar

signs which illustrate both the acceptance of his prayers and the foreknowledge of future events bestowed upon him.

Questions

QUESTION 1: What was the name of the boy who developed the signs of hydrophobia?

YOUR RESPONSE: _____

_____

QUESTION 2: Where was he taken?

YOUR RESPONSE: _____

_____

QUESTION 3: What was the reply of the doctors when the symptoms of rabies reoccurred?

YOUR RESPONSE: _____

_____

QUESTION 4: Why was Hazrat Ahmad[as] perturbed?

YOUR RESPONSE: _____
_____
_____
_____

A DEBATE WITH CHRISTIANS

Before Hazrat Ahmad's[as] time, the Christians of India used to launch strong attacks against Islam and its teachings. They used to take advantage of some false Traditions which had crept into Islamic literature and erroneous beliefs which Muslims of that time had wrongly attributed to Islam. The result was that the Christian missionaries had great success in converting Muslims to Christianity. Not only the masses, but also some learned scholars among Muslims renounced their religion and joined the fold of Christianity. Rev. Abdullah Atham was one such scholar. He was a civil servant, and after retirement from the service, he devoted most of his time to upholding the cause of Christianity and denouncing Islam.

Seeing the sad plight of Islam, Hazrat Ahmad[as] rose to the occasion and not only defended Islam against all attacks but also challenged other religions to expound the beauties of their faiths as compared to Islam.

Rev. Abdullah Atham accepted the challenge and a debate was arranged at Amritsar which continued for fifteen days, an account of which was published under the title *Jang-e-Muqaddas* (Holy War). In this debate, as in all others, victory remained with Hazrat Ahmad[as].

The debate was conducted in writing. Each side had to read out the paper it had written to the audience. Hazrat Ahmad[as] asked for and was granted an important principle; that the arguments presented by the parties in favour of their claims must be taken only from their holy scriptures. Several times during the course of discussion, the powerful arguments of Hazrat Ahmad[as] cornered Christian advocates and compelled them to retreat from their arguments.

One day, a curious episode occurred during the session. The Christians had collected a number of maimed lepers, and blind people, and in order to embarrass Hazrat Ahmad[as], they brought them together before him. Rev. Abdullah Atham, while reading his speech, addressed Hazrat Ahmad[as] and said, 'Jesus[as] used to heal the lepers, the blind and the maimed. You claim to be the Promised Messiah[as]. Heal these people to prove your claim.' The people present there were intrigued as to how Hazrat Ahmad[as] would deal with the situation.

When it was the turn of Hazrat Ahmad[as] to read out his speech, he thanked the Christians for gathering these sufferers and told them that the healing of such patients by Jesus[as] was a claim made by the Bible. It was the Bible which

says that Jesus[as] used to cure the sick by the mere touch of his hands and not by medicine or by prayer.

As for him, the miracles of Jesus[as] were subject to an altogether different interpretation. He also told them that it is written in the Scriptures that if the followers of Jesus[as] had true faith equal to a mustard grain, they could perform more wonderful miracles than the mere healing of sick people. Hazrat Ahmad[as] continued on to say that, therefore, it was the Christians who should come forward themselves, if they had in them faith as little as the grain of mustard seed, and place their hands on the sick people and command them to be whole. If they succeeded in curing them, everyone would be convinced of their truth. If, however, they failed then no one could possibly believe that they were true in their claims.

When the Christians heard this reply, they were dumbfounded and hastened to change the topic.

During this controversy, the attitude of Rev. Abdullah Atham became grossly insulting to the Holy Prophet[saw] of Islam. Hazrat Ahmad[as] tried in vain to remind him of the conditions of the debate and to stop ridiculing the Holy Prophet[saw]. He told him that if he did not stop using foul language, he would be punished by God; but the Christian spokesman did not care. Hazrat Ahmad[as] prayed to God and was told that Abdullah Atham would receive the punishment within 15 months if he did not repent. The heated dialogue was still on when Hazrat Ahmad^{as} told the people what was revealed to him.

When Abdullah Atham heard the warning, he was terrified. For fifteen months after the debate, he did not utter or write a single word against the Holy Prophet^{saw}. These were clear indications that he had repented at heart and inclined towards truth. So, as laid down in the prophecy, God Almighty granted him some respite. The opponents of Hazrat Ahmad^{as}, however, raised a hue and cry. They said that the prophecy had failed. Atham had not been punished.

When Hazrat Ahmad^{as} came to know about this, he offered a cash reward of Rs 4000, if Atham would declare, on oath, that he had not been impressed by the truth of Islam at all. He added that if he took such an oath, he would die within a year, and if he did no such thing, even then God would not let him go unpunished.

Atham did not take the oath. However, within the specified period of time, he died on 27th July, 1896 and provided a sign of the victory of Islam.

Questions:

QUESTION 1: Why did Christian missionaries succeed in converting Muslims into Christianity?

YOUR RESPONSE: _____

_____

QUESTION 2: What did the Promised Messiah[as] do when presented the maimed lepers and blind people? Why was Atham terrified?

YOUR RESPONSE: _____

_____

QUESTION 3: What happened to Atham that provided a sign of victory for Islam?

YOUR RESPONSE: _____

_____

_____

Hazrat Mirza Ghulam Ahmad of Qadian
The Promised Messiah & Mahdi as

HAZRAT AHMAD[as] IN COURT

In 1897, a Christian missionary, Dr. Henry Martyn Clarke, who was then working in Amritsar, brought a charge against Hazrat Ahmad[as] in the court of the District Magistrate Amritsar. The charge was that Hazrat Ahmad[as] had hired a person called Abdul Hamid to kill Dr. Clarke. This was a very grave charge against Hazrat Ahmad[as]. Abdul Hamid was brought before the court, where he stated that he was sent by Ahmad[as] to kill the Christian missionary. The District Magistrate, Mr Martineau, immediately issued a warrant for the arrest of Hazrat Ahmad[as].

The news of the warrant of arrest spread fast and brought joy and jubilation in the enemy's camp. Many of them would gather everyday at Amritsar railway station in the hope of seeing Hazrat Ahmad[as] handcuffed when brought back from Qadian by the police, so that they could jeer at him, mock at his claim of Messiahship and try to humiliate him, if they had the chance. But their dream did not come true, as the warrant was never served on Hazrat Ahmad[as]. In fact, the District Magistrate discovered that he had no jurisdiction to issue such a warrant, as the offence charged was alleged to have been committed in Gurdaspur district. Therefore, he transferred the case to the court of the District Magistrate Gurdaspur. This office was held at the time by a certain Captain Douglas.

In this case, all the enemies of Hazrat Ahmad[as], whether they were Hindus, Christians or Muslims, joined together and left no stone unturned to try and put him in jail. An Aryah Samaj lawyer offered his services to the Christian missionaries to conduct the case free of charge on their behalf. Several Muslim Maulawis also volunteered their help to give evidence against Hazrat Ahmad[as]. Maulawi Muhammad Hussain of Batala was one of these who appeared as a witness in the court to support the prosecution story.

When he appeared before Captain Douglas, Abdul Hamid reaffirmed his story that he was sent by Ahmad[as] to kill Dr. Clarke. The District Magistrate summoned Hazrat Ahmad[as] as well and had his statement recorded. Captain Douglas examined the story told by Abdul Hamid before him, and that told by him before the District Magistrate Amritsar, and found many discrepancies in the two statements. He also noted that Abdul Hamid had made one statement one day and the next day had added several details which were missing from the first. This made him suspect that someone was tutoring him. Abdul Hamid was in the care of the Christian mission during the time that he pretended that his life was in danger due to his statement against Hazrat Ahmad[as]. Captain Douglas postponed the case for four weeks and asked the Superintendent of Police to remove Abdul Hamid from the custody of the Christian missionaries in order to record his statement again. As soon as he was brought before the Superintendent of Police and questioned by him, Abdul Hamid fell at his feet crying and confessed that whatever he had said against Hazrat Ahmad[as] was a lie. He was neither sent by Ahmad[as] for the purpose alleged nor had anything to do with him. He told him that he was coerced by some of the employees of the Christian mission to say what he had said in the court. He also disclosed that sometimes these employees used to write on the palm of his hand, so that he could look at it in case he forgot the names and addresses of the people to be mentioned in the statement.

After hearing this confession, Captain Douglas discharged the case and gave an impartial verdict in favour of Hazrat Ahmad[as]. Not only did he discharge Hazrat Ahmad[as] honourably, but he also gave him permission to prosecute the Christian missionaries who had brought a false charge against him. Hazrat Ahmad[as], however, forgave them all and did not start any proceedings against them. Therefore, whereas the Pilate who had tried Jesus Christ showed weakness and swerved from the path of justice when Jesus[as] was brought before him as an accused, Captain Douglas remained firm and did not give in to the pressure of all the enemies of Hazrat Ahmad[as] to punish him.

Two incidents which occurred during the proceedings of this case are worth mentioning here: Maulawi Muhammad Hussain of Batala was a prosecution witness. As he came into the court room to give evidence against Hazrat Ahmad[as], he saw the latter sitting in a chair, which had been provided for him by the court as a gesture of respect. He was immediately jealous of this and demanded a chair for himself as well. The court refused. Maulawi Muhammad Hussain insisted that a chair should be given to him as one had been given to Hazrat Ahmad[as]. At this Captain Douglas said to him, 'Will you shut up and stand erect in the witness box.' After giving evidence, Maulawi Sahib came out and tried to sit on a chair in the veranda of the courtroom but was told to move on by the orderly of the court, who was not happy with the evidence given by him in court. Maulawi Muhammad Hussain was a well-known scholar among Muslims, though he was an arch enemy of Hazrat

Ahmad^{as}. He was anxious to learn the result of the proceedings, so he approached a group of people who were sitting outside also waiting to hear the result. One of them offered him a cloth sheet to sit on, little suspecting that Maulawi Sahib had come to assist the prosecution, but, when he came to know the purpose of his visit, he too requested him to leave. Thus, Maulawi Muhammad Hussain, who had come to see Hazrat Ahmad^{as} being humiliated, was humiliated himself.

Again, during the proceeding, when the counsel appearing on behalf of Hazrat Ahmad^{as} put a question in cross-examination to Maulawi Muhammad Hussain, which related to the mother of the witness and the answer to which would have humiliated him, Hazrat Ahmad^{as} stopped his counsel, saying:

> I will not allow such a question to be put as I have no desire to heap shame upon him.

Everyone in the court room was quietly impressed by the magnanimity of Hazrat Ahmad^{as}.

Even his lawyer, Mr Fazal Din, who was not an Ahmadi, remarked with surprise after the case. 'Ahmad^{as} is a wonderful person; an opponent attacks his honour, puts his life in jeopardy, and in return he stops his lawyer from asking his opponent such questions as might discredit the evidence.'

Questions

QUESTION 1: What was the name of the Christian missionary that bought a charge against Hazrat Ahmad[as]?

YOUR RESPONSE: _____

_____

QUESTION 2: What was the basis of the charge?

YOUR RESPONSE: _____

_____

_____

QUESTION 3: Who was the judge that heard the case?

YOUR RESPONSE: _____

QUESTION 4: What did Hazrat Ahmad's[as] lawyer say in regard to Hazrat Ahmad's[as] conduct?

YOUR RESPONSE:

QUESTION 5: What was the verdict of the case and on what basis did the judge reach the verdict?

YOUR RESPONSE:

THE DAGGER OF MUHAMMAD^{saw}

The 6th of March recalls memories of a magnificent sign which appeared in the year 1897 for the glory of Islam. The leaders of a new Hindu sect called Aryah Samaj started a campaign to persuade the Muslims to abandon their faith and join the fold of Hinduism. In order to achieve their objective, they used foul means. They used abusive language against the Holy Prophet[saw] of Islam, and distorted the Quranic verses and Islamic teachings to bias the minds of the people against Islam. One of the leaders of the Aryah Samaj, Lekh Ram by name, was the most daring of all in using obscene language against Islam and its founder. Hazrat Ahmad[as] tried to reason with him and to explain the truth of Islam, but to no effect. Lekh Ram ridiculed him and demanded a heavenly sign for the truth of Islam. Hazrat Ahmad[as] wrote several books answering the objections raised by the Aryah Samaj and warned Lekh Ram of the consequences of the foul language he was using against Islam and its founder. In one of his books, referring to Lekh Ram, he wrote in Persian verse:

Beware, O stupid and misguided enemy and tremble with fear of the sharp dagger of Muhammad^{saw}.

But Lekh Ram did not mend his ways. Hazrat Ahmad^{as} therefore prayed to God and learnt that the end of this man was near. He informed Lekh Ram about the prophecy and offered to withhold publishing it if he had any objection. Lekh Ram replied that he had nothing to fear, and repeatedly challenged Hazrat Ahmad^{as} to publish such a prophecy and agreed that such a prediction would be the sole criterion of the truth or falsehood of Islam if it came true. Hazrat Ahmad^{as} therefore issued a leaflet on 20th February, 1893, in which he announced that Lekh Ram, within six years, would meet a calamity of extraordinary character which would prove fatal for him. He also added words of Arabic revelation relating to him, the translation of which would be, 'He is a lifeless calf from which issues an unpleasant sound; nothing awaits it but disgrace and destruction.'

He also announced that Lekh Ram would be a victim of the dagger of Muhammad^{saw} because of his abuses against the Prophet. He would meet a fate similar to the calf of Samri, i.e. he would be cut into pieces, burnt, and the ashes thrown into water. It would happen on a day close to Eid festival, just before or just after.

Again in April, 1893, he declared that he had seen in a vision a fearful-looking person who was searching for Lekh Ram as if he had been appointed to carry out the punishment.

He also announced that 'if this person is not overtaken within the period of six years by a torment that should be distinguishable from ordinary sufferings and should bear an extraordinary character and should be in the nature of Divine punishment, then it might be concluded that I have not been sent by God Almighty, nor do I speak under the urge of His spirit. If I am proved false in any aspect of this prophecy, I will be ready to undergo any punishment and would be willing that a rope might be drawn around my neck and I might be hanged.'

On 2nd April, 1893, he wrote, 'This morning in the course of a light slumber I saw that I was sitting in a large room where some of my friends were present when a well-built man of terrible appearance came and stood before me. As I looked at him, he asked me: Where is Lekh Ram? He also named another person and inquired where he was. Then I understood that this person standing in front of me had been appointed for the chastisement of Lekh Ram and the other person, whose name I do not remember now, though I am certain that he is one of those whom I have mentioned in my announcement.'

At another point, he announced, 'God has given me the good news and said, "You will recognise the day of joy which will be closest to the day of the Eid festival."' Hazrat Ahmad[as] pointed out that this verse referred to Lekh Ram and that he would meet his fate on the day next to Eid day.

Lekh Ram did not seem to be at all frightened; his language became increasingly objectionable day by day. In reply to the above prophecy of Hazrat Ahmad[as], he predicted that Ahmad[as] instead would die of cholera within three years, for he was an impostor, and announced that this would be a sign of the truth of Aryah Samaj.

At the time that Hazrat Ahmad[as] published this prophecy, he was over fifty years of age while Lekh Ram was only thirty. It so happened that five years after the publication of this prophecy, as the limit described in it was approaching, and doubts about the truth of the prophecy were being raised in some quarters, Lekh Ram was mysteriously attacked in his own house in Lahore. He was stabbed in the stomach with something sharp, severing his entrails at several places, on Saturday 6th March, 1897, which happened to be the day following that of Eid day. The assailant was described as a ferocious looking man who had come to Lekh Ram as a seeker after truth and had stayed with him for some time. While this was happening, Lekh Ram's mother and wife were in an adjoining room. They rushed out immediately to help Lekh Ram. The street was crowded with Hindus. When Lekh Ram cried out for help, they also ran to rescue him, but could not find the attacker. It is alleged that Lekh Ram's mother tried to take hold of the assailant but he struck her on the head and in the confusion that ensued, made his escape from the house. Nobody ever knew who the assailant was, and despite all their efforts, the police could not arrest anyone for his attempted murder.

Lekh Ram died the following day. The doctors performed emergency operations to save him but could not do so. He was cremated and his ashes were thrown into the river according to the Hindu custom.

Lekh Ram's death caused a huge storm in the Hindu world. A terrible hue and cry was raised throughout the country. Meetings were held and resolutions were passed expressing anger and concern. Rewards for the arrest of the assailant were announced. An immediate enquiry was demanded and it was openly suggested that Hazrat Ahmad[as] should be charged with his murder. Threats were also made to his life. The authorities carried out a prompt search of his house, in the hope that some clue to the murder might be found, but failed. God foiled all the attempts of his enemies and, though every effort was made to involve him in the crime, Hazrat Ahmad's[as] innocence was completely and fully established.

The clear fulfilment of this prophecy, in which the Aryah Samaj suffered and Islam triumphed, brought many people into the fold of Ahmadiyyat.

Questions

QUESTION 1: What was the name of the person mentioned in the prophecy?

YOUR RESPONSE:

QUESTION 2: Which Hindu sect did the person belong to?

YOUR RESPONSE:

QUESTION 3: On which date did Hazrat Ahmad[as] publish his prophecy?

YOUR RESPONSE: _____

_____

QUESTION 4: How did Lekh Ram die?

YOUR RESPONSE: _____

_____

_____

_____

_____

_____

QUESTION 5: On which date was the prophecy fulfilled?

YOUR RESPONSE: _____

_____

THE FATE OF SA'DULLAH

Sa'dullah was a teacher at the Mission High School in Ludhiana, a town in Punjab. He was a bitter enemy of Hazrat Ahmad[as]. He used to write poems and articles against Hazrat Ahmad[as] and publish them. His writing was always obscene, filthy, and full of abuse. Hazrat Ahmad[as] had once said that no other prophet had been abused as much by any person as he had been abused by Sa'dullah. Apart from teaching, which was his job, he would spend all his energy in denouncing the Promised Messiah[as]. He used to say that Hazrat Ahmad[as] was an impostor and all his prophecies were a pack of lies, that he would become miserable in the end and would die childless. When Sa'dullah's hostility exceeded all bounds and he became the means of preventing people from seeing the truth, Hazrat Ahmad[as] prayed to God that a sign be shown to this man and his associates.

His prayer was heard and he received a revelation about the future of Sa'dullah, the translation of which is, 'Your enemy who said that you shall be childless, shall himself be cut off and his line will become extinct.'

Hazrat Ahmad[as] informed Sa'dullah about this revelation. He also wrote a book regarding this whole affair in the hope that he would repent for what he had done and thus save himself from God's wrath, but to no effect. Sa'dullah continued using abusive language against Hazrat Ahmad[as].

At the time of the prophecy, Sa'dullah was in good health and in the prime of his youth. He had a son who was nearly fourteen years of age. Sa'dullah lived for a further fifteen years after this prophecy, but no more children were born to him. He died in 1907, but the matter did not end there, as the opponents of Hazrat Ahmad[as] began to say that the prophecy had not been fulfilled since Sa'dullah had left a son who survived him. Hazrat Ahmad[as] replied that as Sa'dullah's son was in existence at the time of revelation, his surviving Sa'dullah did not affect the truth of the prophecy. He again affirmed that the young man would not have any children and that Sa'dullah's line would certainly become extinct as revealed to him by God.

When Hazrat Ahmad[as] published this reply concerning Sa'dullah's son, one of his followers cautioned him against the publication of such a prediction on the ground that if a child was born to the young man, Hazrat Ahmad[as] would find himself in an awkward position and that he might run the risk of criminal prosecution. Hazrat Ahmad[as] replied that he could neither doubt nor reject that which God had revealed to him, and that his disciple's caution was due to his weak faith. In the end, it turned out that the same disciple broke away from the community after the death of Hazrat Ahmad[as].

It so happened that although Hazrat Ahmad's[as] opponents persuaded Sa'dullah's son to marry twice in the hope that he might have a son and so falsify the prophecy, no children were born to him.

Thus Sa'dullah and his son earned God's wrath by insisting on the use of filthy and obscene language against the prophet of the age.

Questions

QUESTION 1: Who was Sa'dullah?

YOUR RESPONSE: _____

_____

QUESTION 2: When did the Promised Messiah[as] pray for a sign to be shown to Sa'dullah and company?

YOUR RESPONSE: _____

_____

QUESTION 3: What was the prophecy regarding Sa'dullah's bloodline?

YOUR RESPONSE: _____

_____

_____

_____

_____

QUESTION 4: What was the result of Sa'dullah's abuse of the Promised Messiah[as]?

YOUR RESPONSE: _____

_____

_____

_____

_____

THE TRUTH PREVAILS

Once, Hazrat Ahmad[as] wrote an article in support of Islam and sent it to Wakeel Press at Amritsar, a town in the province of Punjab, India, for publication. The owner of the Press was a fanatic Christian called Rallia Ram and was a lawyer by profession. The manuscript was sent in a packet open at both ends and stamped at the reduced rate prescribed for postal packets. Hazrat Ahmad[as] also enclosed a letter in it addressed to Rallia Ram giving him instructions about the article.

Sending a letter in a packet at a much lower rate of charge was against the Post Office regulations in those days. It was an offence punishable with a fine of up to 500 rupees, or with imprisonment for up to six months. Hazrat Ahmad[as], however, knew nothing of this regulation.

Rallia Ram, being an opponent of Islam, made a complaint against Hazrat Ahmad[as] to the Postal authorities and a case was filed in the court against Hazrat Ahmad[as]. He was then summoned to appear in court at Gurdaspur, the headquarters of the District, on a charge of defrauding the Post Office. Hazrat Ahmad's[as] lawyer, Shaikh Ali Ahmad, advised him to deny that he had placed the letter in the packet and suggested that Hazrat Ahmad[as] should make a statement in the court that Rallia Ram himself might have done it so as to get Hazrat Ahmad[as] into trouble. 'This is the only way out!', He said. Hazrat Ahmad[as] rejected his advice and said that under no circumstance would he make a false statement. 'You are bound to be convicted and punished if you do not heed my advice,' said Shaikh Ali Ahmad. Hazrat Ahmad[as], however, was determined not to lie. His lawyer therefore refused to defend him and so Hazrat Ahmad[as] conducted his own defence.

The magistrate in whose court he appeared was European, as was the Superintendent of the Post Office who represented the prosecution. The magistrate asked Hazrat Ahmad[as] whether he had placed the letter in the packet and sent it to Rallia Ram. Hazrat Ahmad[as] replied that he was not aware of this specific regulation, but he had placed the letter in the packet and despatched it to Rallia Ram. He explained that it was not a private letter; it only contained instructions as to how the article was to be printed. He assured the court that he had no intention of defrauding the Post Office. The Post Office's Superintendent was adamant that Hazrat Ahmad's[as] statement amounted to a confession of the crime and that he should be punished according to the law. The

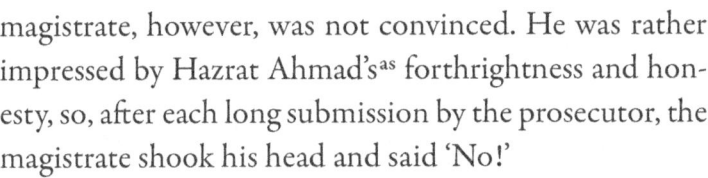

magistrate, however, was not convinced. He was rather impressed by Hazrat Ahmad's[as] forthrightness and honesty, so, after each long submission by the prosecutor, the magistrate shook his head and said 'No!'

Hazrat Ahmad[as] was thus acquitted and the case was dropped in spite of the strong opposition from the prosecution.

Questions

QUESTION 1: To which Press did Hazrat Ahmad[as] send the article to be printed?

YOUR RESPONSE: _____

_____

QUESTION 2: Who was the owner of the Press?

YOUR RESPONSE: _____

_____

QUESTION 3: Why did the owner of the Press file a case against Hazrat Ahmad[as]?

YOUR RESPONSE: _____

_____

QUESTION 4: Where was the case heard?

YOUR RESPONSE: _____

_____

QUESTION 5: What suggestion did his Lawyer make to Hazrat Ahmad[as]?

YOUR RESPONSE: _____

_____

QUESTION 6: Why did Hazrat Ahmad[as] reject the advice of his Lawyer?

YOUR RESPONSE: _____

_____

QUESTION 7: What was the outcome of the case?

YOUR RESPONSE: _____

_____

_____

_____

QUESTION 8: What lesson do you draw from this episode?

YOUR RESPONSE: _____

_____

_____

_____

_____

_____

_____

_____

A HINDU TRIES TO HYPNOTISE HAZRAT AHMAD[as]

A Hindu man came to Qadian with a marriage party. He was a great expert in hypnotism. During his stay in Qadian, he said to his friends that they should all go and visit Hazrat Ahmad[as]. The idea that he had in mind was to try and hypnotise Hazrat Ahmad[as] and make him do something disgraceful in the presence of his followers. It should be remembered that hypnotism is a powerful yet delicate science; with proper training and concentration, it can be developed to a remarkable degree so as to influence the behaviour of any person on whom it is exercised.

The Hindu man found Hazrat Ahmad[as] sitting in a mosque with some of his companions. He went in quietly, sat in the back row, and started to hypnotise Hazrat Ahmad[as]. Hazrat Ahmad[as] continued his talk undisturbed. After a short time, the Hindu gentleman began trembling with fear. He pulled himself together and again concentrated on trying to hypnotise Hazrat Ahmad[as], but he could not continue. He screamed in terror and ran out of the mosque onto the street.

The people inside the mosque followed him into the street in order to find out what the matter was. He told them that he had tried to hypnotise Hazrat Ahmad[as], and while concentrating on Hazrat Ahmad[as], he saw not Hazrat Ahmad[as], but a lion in his place. He trembled with fear but soon gathered himself with the reassurance that it was nothing but a hallucination on his part. When he tried for the second time he again saw the lion, but this time the ferocious animal was advancing towards him. He was again terrified but did not lose heart. At the third attempt, he saw the lion ready to pounce upon him, at which point he ran out of the mosque to save his life.

The people let him go and thus yet another attempt to disgrace Hazrat Ahmad[as] was foiled.

Questions

QUESTION 1: What was the plan of the Hindu man?

YOUR RESPONSE: _____

_____

QUESTION 2: What did he see when he attempted to hypnotise Hazrat Ahmad[as]?

YOUR RESPONSE: _____

_____

_____

_____

_____

QUESTION 3: Why did he run away from the mosque?

YOUR RESPONSE: _____

_____

_____

_____

_____

_____

Mian Abdullah[ra] holding Ahmad's[as] shirt with red ink

AND GOD SIGNED IN RED INK

One day, whilst resting, Hazrat Ahmad[as] had a vision in which it appeared that he had prepared a chart relating to some future events in his own life and in the lives of some of his friends, which he desired God to approve. He saw in his vision that he was sitting before God, so he placed the chart before his Lord for his signature. God took his pen, dipped it into the inkpot, flicked the surplus ink from the tip of the nib with a movement of his hand, and signed the chart. Hazrat Ahmad[as] noticed that it was red ink that his lord flicked and signed with.

Mian Muhammad Abdullah Sanauri[ra] was sitting near to Hazrat Ahmad[as] whilst Hazrat Ahmad[as] was resting. He was gently massaging the feet of Hazrat Ahmad[as] when, all of a sudden, he noticed that Hazrat Ahmad[as] began to tremble in his sleep. He then noticed some ink drops fall onto Hazrat Ahmad's[as] clothes and also onto his own cap. Mian Abdullah[ra] did not know what was happening. He was surprised to see the wet ink drops on the shirt of Hazrat Ahmad[as] and wondered where they had come from as there was no inkpot in the room.

He looked up at the roof, but it was smooth and clean. He searched around the room but could find absolutely nowhere that the ink could have come from.

After a little while, when Hazrat Ahmad[as] woke up he related his vision to Mian Abdullah[ra] and told him that the ink stains on his clothes were a proof of God's existence. Mian Abdullah[ra] very humbly requested that the shirt be given to him as he had the privilege to witness this miracle. Hazrat Ahmad[as] gave him the shirt on condition that he must direct in his will that the shirt should be buried along with his body, lest people should begin to worship it.

Mian Abdullah[ra] kept the shirt dear to his heart as long as he lived and thousands of people saw it, but when he died in 1927, the shirt was buried along with him in accordance to his will. This episode was in fact a symbolic representation of the close relationship which Hazrat Ahmad[as] had with Allah.

Questions

QUESTION 1: What was the name of the companion of Hazrat Ahmad[as] who was with him during this miracle?

YOUR RESPONSE: _____

_____

QUESTION 2: What was Hazrat Ahmad[as] doing whilst this miracle occurred?

YOUR RESPONSE: _____

_____

QUESTION 3: What instructions were given to the companion regarding the shirt?

YOUR RESPONSE: _____

_____

Sahibzada Abdul Lateef[ra]

TWO GREAT MARTYRS

Hazrat Ahmad[as] received a revelation from God that

Two goats would be slaughtered.

Hazrat Ahmad[as] interpreted this dream to mean that two innocent people amongst his companions would be killed unjustly. The prophecy was fulfilled through the martyrdom of Sahibzada Abdul Lateef[ra] and Maulawi Abdur-Rehman[ra], both in Kabul, Afghanistan.

Sahibzada Sayed Abdul Lateef[ra] was a descendant of the well known Muslim saint Hazrat Sheikh Abdul Hasan Ali Hajveri. His hometown was in the province of Khost in Afghanistan. His father was the chief of the tribe and owned about 30,000 acres of land in his village of Saidgah and also in Bannu. Sahibzada Abdul Lateef was educated in a religious school and was well known for his piety, integrity, and his knowledge of Islam. He was held in such high esteem that the ruler of Afghanistan, Abdur-Rehman Khan, asked Sahibzada Abdul Lateef[ra] to tutor his son Habibullah Khan. He was one of two members of the Afghan government who were part of a delegation during negotiations with the British over territorial rights. During the course of these discussions, he came across an Ahmadi clerk, Sayed Chan Badshah, who told him about Hazrat Ahmad[as] and his claim to be the Promised Messiah[as]. Sahibzada Abdul Lateef was very excited as he had also received revelations from God that the time of the Mahdi was imminent. Sayed Chan Badshah gave Sahibzada Abdul Lateef[ra] one of the Promised Messiah's[as] books to read, *Aa'eenah-e-Kamaalaat-e-Islam*. That book changed the life of Sahibzada Abdul Lateef; as he remained absorbed in reading it all night and was totally convinced that Hazrat Ahmad[as], the author, was indeed the Promised Messiah[as].

Sahibzada Abdul Lateef was most anxious to establish contact with Hazrat Ahmad[as], so as soon as he returned to Kabul from the negotiations with the British he sent one of his most trusted followers, Maulawi Abdur-Rehman, to Qadian to meet with Hazrat Ahmad[as] and to hand him a letter of *bai'at*. Maulawi Abdur-Rehman met the Promised Messiah[as] and stayed in Qadian for some time. He continued to visit Qadian on a number of occasions and would always take back books for Sahibzada Abdul Lateef[ra].

On his return to Kabul from one of his visits to

Qadian, Maulawi Abdur-Rehman had in his possession some pamphlets which contained the true Islamic teachings about jihad. At that time, there was a lot of agitation in the Frontier areas against the British, which was described by the Afghan mullahs to be a jihad. Hazrat Ahmad[as] had condemned this violence against the British in his pamphlets. Upon reaching Kabul, Maulawi Abdur Rehman made public his views on jihad, and was immediately arrested and put into prison for daring to criticize the Afghan Mullahs. He was subsequently strangled to death on the orders of the Amir of Afghanistan, Abdur Rehman. He thus became the first martyr from among the followers Hazrat Ahmad[as]. A few weeks later, the Amir felt the wrath of God. He suffered a severe paralytic stroke and died shortly after.

Towards the end of 1902, Sahibzada Abdul Lateef[ra] set out from Kabul with the intention of performing Hajj. He had also planned to travel to Qadian and finally meet the Promised Messiah[as]. He had intended to stop for only a few days in Qadian, but upon meeting Hazrat Ahmad[as], he was so greatly affected that he ended up staying for several months.

When the time came for him to leave and head back to Kabul, the Promised Messiah[as] accompanied him for many miles outside of Qadian. The moment of separation was very painful for Sahibzada Abdul Lateef[ra], he was already convinced through dreams that he would never see the Promised Messiah[as] again and that on his return to Kabul, he would have to lay down his life in the cause of truth. He had told his friends in Qadian, 'After I have been martyred you should go and tell the Promised Messiah[as].'

Soon after his arrival, many chiefs came to welcome the Sahibzada as they were under the impression that he had returned after performing Hajj. He explained to them that he had stopped in Qadian and met the Promised Messiah, Hazrat Ahmad[as], and that he had accepted the truth of the Promised Messiah[as]. On hearing this news, the Amir, Habibullah Khan had Sahibzada Abdul Lateef[ra] arrested and put in prison. This was the same Habibullah that had been taught by Sahibzada Abdul Lateef[ra] and on whose coronation had asked Sahibzada Abdul Lateef[ra] to perform the ceremony.

In prison he was chained hand and foot, and was kept in prison for approximately four months. He was constantly told to refute his belief in the Promised Messiah[as] and thus save his own life, but Sahibzada Abdul Lateef[ra] remained true to his beliefs. The Amir asked Sahibzada Abdul Lateef[ra] to think about what would happen to Sahibzada's young family and all of his property should he be executed, but again Sahibzada Abdul Lateef[ra] put his full faith in Allah to look after his family and did not back down from the truth about the Promised Messiah[as].

Sahibzada Abdul Lateef[ra] was sentenced to be stoned to death on the 14th of July, 1903. He was led through the crowded streets in chains and taken to the place of execution. On the way, he was asked by a Maulawi why he was walking so quickly even with all the chains on him, and Sahibzada Abdul Lateef[ra] replied 'I am walking briskly because I am impatient for a rendezvous with my Master.' There was not the slightest trace of fear on his face when the first stones were thrown by the Amir and the Judge who had sentenced him to die. Sahibzada Abdul Lateef[ra] was martyred whilst reciting a verse of *Surah Yusuf,* 'Thou art my helper in this world and the hereafter. Let death when it comes find me in a state of complete submission to Thy will and join me to the company of the righteous.'

Questions

QUESTION 1: Who was the first martyr of Ahmadiyyat?

YOUR RESPONSE: _____

_____

QUESTION 2: Who was the second martyr of Ahmadiyyat?

YOUR RESPONSE: _____

_____

QUESTION 3: In which country were they martyred?

YOUR RESPONSE: _____

_____

_____

QUESTION 4: When and how was Sahibzada Abdul Lateef[ra] martyred?

YOUR RESPONSE:

THE GIRL WITH SWOLLEN EYES

It is said that Jesus[as] used to cure the sick, the blind, and the lepers with the touch of his hands. In fact, blessing a person with breath or with the touch of fingers accompanied by prayers is a kind of treatment which holy and righteous persons use to demonstrate the power of prayer.

Many instances of this kind are found in the life of the Holy Prophet Muhammad[saw]. For instance, at a time when no other treatment was available, he placed his hand on the ailing eye of a devoted and dear companion and it was immediately cured. On another occasion, when water was badly needed, he put his fingers into the container and his blessed touch caused the small quantity of water to suffice for a large number of people.

Hazrat Ahmad[as] also performed similar miracles. He once helped a small girl whose eyes were so badly swollen that no treatment was effective. He touched her eyes with his fingers and prayed. She was soon completely cured.

Amatullah Bibi was only a child when she migrated from Kabul with her father and uncle to Qadian, the hometown of Hazrat Ahmad[as]. In fact, they were forced to leave the country after the martyrdom of Sahibzada Syed Abdul Lateef[ra], as life was made impossible for Ahmadi Muslims in that land. This poor girl had serious trouble with her eyes; both eyes were so red and swollen that she could not even open them properly. Her parents tried many different treatments, but to no effect. Her condition continued to worsen. One day, when she was only ten years old, she decided to go to Hazrat Ahmad's[as] house to ask for his blessings and help. With tears in her eyes, she begged Hazrat Ahmad[as] to bless her painful eyes with his heavenly breath. Hazrat Ahmad[as] looked at her swollen eyes, took a little saliva from his mouth and applied it to her eyes whilst praying solemnly and silently for her recovery. Then he placed his hand on her head affectionately and said, 'Dear child, go home now. By the grace of God you will recover soon.'

God accepted his prayers and Amatullah Bibi did recover very soon afterwards. She lived for more than sixty years after this incident but never had any trouble with her eyes again.

Questions

QUESTION 1: What was the name of the child cured by Hazrat Ahmad[as]?

YOUR RESPONSE: _____

_____

QUESTION 2: Where did the child and her father come from?

YOUR RESPONSE: _____

_____

QUESTION 3: Why did they leave their country?

YOUR RESPONSE: _____

_____

_____

QUESTION 4: How did Hazrat Ahmad[as] cure the child?

YOUR RESPONSE: _____

_____

_____

_____

ACTIVITIES

ACTIVITY NUMBER ONE

Work out the names of five Holy people mentioned in this book. Once you have worked out the name, find the name on the word board. The arrow will show you which direction each word begins in! The letters must be touching but can be in any direction! Find the names of five Holy People:

1. ↓   AHMAD
2. ←   ~~~~~~~~~~
3. ↗   ~~~~~~~~~~
4. ↓   ~~~~~~~~~~
5. ↗   ~~~~~~~~~~

H	A	A	U	A	S	A	K
D	N	H	M	B	S	U	N
D	A	N	A	K	E	R	H
U	B	D	A	J	K	I	S

ACTIVITY NUMBER TWO

Translate the titles of the following books of the Promised Messiah[as] into English:

BOOKS OF THE PROMISED MESSIAH[AS]

Original Title	English Translation
1 Al-Wasiyyat	The Will
2 Paighaam-e-Sulah	
3 Satt Bachan	
4 Masih Hindustaan Mein	
5 Khutbah Ilhaamiyyah	
6 Aa'eenah-e-Kamaalaat-e-Islam	

Extension: Do you remember what the book was about? Write down a sentence about the book next to the English translation on the grid above.

ACTIVITY NUMBER THREE

Find and insert a check mark:

1. 4 religious groups ☑ ☐ ☐ ☐

2. 4 religious books ☐ ☐ ☐ ☐

3. 6 Holy people ☐ ☐ ☐ ☐
   ☐ ☐

4. 11 places ☐ ☐ ☐ ☐ ☐
   ☐ ☐ ☐ ☐ ☐
   ☐

ACTIVITY NUMBER FOUR

Hidden in the puzzle below are 25 terms used in this book. These words may be spelled vertically, horizontally, backwards, or diagonally. Find these words from the list provided on the next page.

B	K	S	X	E	A	W	M	E	I	S	B	A	Z	A
J	I	A	R	C	T	U	X	S	H	N	A	H	S	M
Q	O	H	C	I	H	O	T	S	A	A	T	D	N	R
B	A	E	A	A	N	S	K	N	Q	I	A	D	O	I
D	M	D	M	S	I	A	H	L	I	T	L	U	V	T
B	A	M	I	H	H	S	G	M	A	S	A	B	E	S
N	A	M	D	A	I	T	A	A	J	I	P	I	D	A
D	K	D	H	R	N	G	N	M	R	R	S	M	A	R
Q	U	N	K	A	B	U	L	A	M	H	R	S	S	W
B	S	M	I	L	S	U	M	E	R	C	I	U	Z	S
H	I	N	D	U	S	Q	D	X	Z	G	M	S	Z	W
E	R	O	H	A	L	I	U	I	K	A	H	E	H	S
E	L	B	I	B	N	R	H	R	G	U	S	J	T	F
T	A	L	W	A	N	D	I	N	A	N	A	K	H	O
D	G	S	M	Q	C	O	J	G	U	N	K	G	F	G

Christians
Muslims
Hindus
Buddhists
Qadian
Batala
Sialkot
Talwandi
Mecca
Muhammad
Medina
Lahore
Kashmir
Kabul
Srinagar
Amritsar
Quran
Vedas
Granth Sahib
Ahmad
Bible
Buddha
Jesus
Nanak
Krishna

ACTIVITY NUMBER FIVE

On the space provided below describe what you imagine that the time looked like when ignorance prevailed all around. On the right side, describe what you imagine the Promised Messiah's[as] upbringing was like during this period—you can use words or images, or a combination of both.

THE TIME WHEN
THE PROMISED MESSIAH[as] WAS BORN

THE PROMISED MESSIAH's[as] UPBRINGING

ACTIVITY NUMBER SIX

In a vision, the Promised Messiah[as] was granted the following words of the Holy Quran by way of revelation:

اَلَيْسَ اللّٰهُ بِكَافٍ عَبْدَهٗ

Is God not sufficient for His servant?

Using the above Arabic text, write in the space provided below in beautiful calligraphy.

ACTIVITY NUMBER SEVEN

There was a popular belief amongst Muslims that Jesus was still alive in the heavens. Write your response showing that Jesus was no longer alive and that he died a natural death, you can use your notes from the previous activity for this too. Make sure you include the following words:

Kashmir	Nebuchad-nezzar	Palestine	Masih Hindustaan Mein	Wounds

Your response: _____

_____

_____

_____

_____

_____

ACTIVITY NUMBER EIGHT

Use the chart below to help explain the beliefs held by Christians, Muslims and Ahmadi Muslims concerning the death of Jesus[as].

Death of Jesus[as]

Christian Beliefs	Non-Ahmadi Muslim Beliefs

Ahmadi Muslim Beliefs

ACTIVITY NUMBER NINE

The Promised Messiah's opponents criticized him for not being well versed in the Arabic language. What did God do about this?

YOUR RESPONSE: _____

_____

_____

_____

YOUR RESPONSE: _____

_____

_____

YOUR RESPONSE: _____

_____

_____

ACTIVITY NUMBER TEN

The Promised Messiah[as] had numerous opponents, many of whom tried to publicly ridicule him, disgrace him and even have him imprisoned. As is the promise of Allah the Almighty to all His Prophets, Allah will always be their Protector. The case was always the same with the Promised Messiah[as]; not a single opponent was successful in their devious plans.

Match the names/descriptions of some of the opponents of the Promised Messiah[as] with what they did:

MATCH THE NAMES WITH DESCRIPTION

Name	Description
Rallia Ram	Tried to hypnotise the Promised Messiah[as] in the presence of this followers and make him do something disgraceful.
An unnamed Hindu man	A Christian Missionary that brought the charge to a court in the District Magistrate of Amritsar, that the Promised Messiah[as] had hired a person to kill him.
Sa'dullah	One of the leaders of Aryah Samaj that constantly used foul language against the Holy Prophet[saw]. This person predicted that the Promised Messiah[as] would die of cholera within a given time period.
Dr. Henry Martyn Clarke	He made a complaint against the Promised Messiah[as] to the postal authorities which resulted in a case being filed against him.
Lekh Ram	He used to write insulting and abusive poems and articles against Hazrat Ahmad[as] and publish them.

ANSWERS TO ACTIVITIES

ACTIVITY NUMBER ONE

H	A	A	U	A	S	A	K
D		H	M	B	S	U	N
D			A		E	R	H
U	B	D	A	J	K	I	S

1. ↓   AHMAD
2. ←   BUDDHA
3. ↗   JESUS
4.   NANAK
5. ↗   KRISHNA

ACTIVITY NUMBER TWO

	Original Title	English Translation
1	Al-Wasiyyat	The Will
2	Paighaam-e-Sulah	The Message of Peace
3	Satt Bachan	True Word
4	Masih Hindustaan Mein	Jesus in India
5	Khutbah Ilhaamiyyah	The Revealed Sermon
6	Aa'eenah-c-Kamaalaat-e-Islam	The Mirror of the Excellences of Islam

ACTIVITY NUMBER THREE

1. 4 Religious Groups: Christians, Muslims, Hindus, Buddhists
2. 4 Religious Books: Quran, Vedas, Granth Sahib, Bible
3. 6 Holy People: Ahmad, Buddha, Jesus, Nanak, Krishna, Muhammad
4. 11 Places: Qadian, Batala, Sialkot, Talwandi, Mecca, Medina, Lahore, Kashmir, Srinagar, Amritsar, Kabul

ACTIVITY NUMBER FOUR

B	K	S	X	E	A	W	M	E	I	S	B	A	Z	A
J	I	A	R	C	T	U	X	S	H	N	A	H	S	M
Q	O	H	C	I	H	O	T	S	A	A	T	D	N	R
B	A	E	A	A	N	S	K	N	Q	I	A	D	O	I
D	M	D	M	S	I	A	H	L	I	T	L	U	V	T
B	A	M	I	H	H	S	G	M	A	S	A	B	E	S
N	A	M	D	A	I	T	A	A	J	I	P	I	D	A
D	K	D	H	R	N	G	N	M	R	R	S	M	A	R
Q	U	N	K	A	B	U	L	A	M	H	R	S	S	W
B	S	M	I	L	S	U	M	E	R	C	I	U	Z	S
H	I	N	D	U	S	Q	D	X	Z	G	M	S	Z	W
E	R	O	H	A	L	I	U	I	K	A	H	E	H	S
E	L	B	I	B	N	R	H	R	G	U	S	J	T	F
T	A	L	W	A	N	D	I	N	A	N	A	K	H	O
D	G	S	M	Q	C	O	J	G	U	N	K	G	F	G

ACTIVITY NUMBER NINE

1. Allah taught the Promised Messiah[as] 40,000 root words of the Arabic language over night

2. Under Divine Command, the Promised Messiah[as] wrote a chapter in Arabic in one of his books

3. In 1900, on the occasion of Eid-ul-Azhaa, God commanded the Promised Messiah[as] to deliver the sermon in the Arabic language.

ACTIVITY NUMBER TEN

Rallia Ram	Tried to hypnotise the Promised Messiah[as] in the presence of this followers and make him do something disgraceful.
An unnamed Hindu man	A Christian Missionary that brought the charge to a court in the District Magistrate of Amritsar, that the Promised Messiah[as] had hired a person to kill him.
Sa'dullah	One of the leaders of Aryah Samaj that constantly used foul language against the Holy Prophet[saw]. This person predicted that the Promised Messiah[as] would die of cholera within a given time period.
Dr. Henry Martyn Clarke	He made a complaint against the Promised Messiah[as] to the postal authorities which resulted in a case being filed against him.
Lekh Ram	He used to write insulting and abusive poems and articles against Hazrat Ahmad[as] and publish them.

PUBLISHER'S NOTE

We have added the references to the Holy Quran citing the name of the *surah* [i.e. chapter], followed by a chapter:verse citation, e.g., Surah al-Jumu'ah, 62:4.

Salutations are recited out of respect when mentioning the names of Prophets and holy personages. These salutations have been abbreviated and inserted into the text where applicable.

Readers are urged to recite the full salutations for the following abbreviations:

- saw *sallallaahu 'alaihi wa sallam,* meaning 'peace and blessings of Allah be upon him', is written after the name of the Holy Prophet Muhammad^{saw}.

- as *'alaihis-salaam,* meaning 'peace be on him', is written after the names of Prophets other than the Holy Prophet Muhammad^{saw}.

- ra *raziyallaahu 'anhu/'anhaa/'anhum,* meaning 'Allah be pleased with him/her/them', is written after the names of the Companions of the Holy Prophet Muhammad^{saw} or of the Promised Messiah^{as}.

rta *rahmatullaah 'alaihi/'alaihaa/'alaihim*, meaning 'Allah shower His mercy upon him/her/them', is written after the names of those deceased pious Muslims who are not Companions of the Holy Prophet Muhammad[saw] or of the Promised Messiah[as].

www.ingramcontent.com/pod-product-compliance
Lightning Source LLC
LaVergne TN
LVHW011719060526
838200LV00051B/2956